When Was Jesus Born?

Misconceptions and Embellishments in the Christmas Story

Andrew Freeland

Revised 2015 edition
© 2014, 2015 by Andrew Freeland

Everyone is permitted to copy and redistribute this material in any medium or format, remix, transform, and build upon this material for any purpose, even commercially. Provided, appropriate credit is given and you do so in any reasonable manner, but not in any way that suggests the licensor endorses you or your use. If you remix, transform, or build upon the material, you must distribute your contributions under the same license as the original.

The Blurb-provided layout designs and graphic elements are copyright Blurb Inc., 2012. This book was created using the Blurb creative publishing service. The book author retains sole copyright to his or her contributions to this book.

The scripture quotations contained herein are from THE HOLY BIBLE, NEW INTERNATIONAL VERSION®, NIV® Copyright © 1973, 1978,1 984, 2011 by Biblica, Inc.® Used by permission. All rights reserved worldwide.
Scripture quotations marked (KJV) are taken from the KING JAMES VERSION.
Scripture quotations marked (ASV) are taken from the AMERICAN STANDARD VERSION.

Front cover painting: *The Adoration of the Shepherds* by Gerard van Honthorst, 1622
Back cover and above photographs by Andrew Freeland

To order copies of this book please visit blurb.com

I would like to give a big thank you to Mom for helping me complete this project. I also want to say *Merry Christmas* to all my family. To everyone at the Gadsden Church of Christ: *God Bless*.

For unto you is born this day in the city of David a Saviour, which is Christ the Lord.

-Luke 2:11 (KJV)

Preface

Throughout this presentation of misconceptions and embellishments in the Christmas story, I tried to stay as true to the scriptures as possible. We are told in Deuteronomy 4:2 and Revelation 22:18 not to add to God's word. Nevertheless, it seems like a lot of adding goes into the story of Jesus' birth. Many elements in the Christmas story differ from the Biblical narrative.

It is the Christmas story, not the Bible, which says that Jesus was born on the 25th of December. Only the Christmas story says the wise men visited Jesus in the manger. The grumpy innkeeper who told Joseph there was no vacancy and to stay in a stable is not found in the Bible. These and other extra details turn the Biblical story, which is a part of God's word, into the Christmas story.

In order to get back to the heart of the scriptures, I wanted to analyze these misconceptions and embellishments. These elements, much like the holiday celebration itself, have gone through centuries of development. The history of Christmas not only predates the establishment of the Church, but goes back many years before Jesus was even born. Not only are non-scriptural elements added to the nativity story, most Christmas traditions are rooted in pagan worship. Little of what we do at Christmas is actually a part of the Bible.

Of course, the hardest part to research was: when exactly *was* Jesus born? Many historians and theologians have attributed a lot of different dates and years to Jesus' birth. Among all the theories, I have found that the ones included in this book are the most consistent with the scriptures. The exact time of the nativity is not expressed in the verses. However, the Bible does present enough clues in order to make an educated assumption. (And guess what? It wasn't in December).

The Shepherds and the Angel
Carl Bloch
1879

Introduction

Christmas is a world wide holiday celebrated in December by millions of people. For many people, it is their favorite time of year. Nowadays, Christmas seems to have expanded past a single day, with festivities beginning earlier and earlier. It is a time for get-togethers with family, the giving of gifts, good food, and a holiday spirit that only comes once a year. It is also the time when many Christians remember the birth of Jesus Christ.

Every December there is a bombardment of nativity themed movies and documentaries, Christmas pageants, nativity scenes in front of various churches, and so much more. Throughout all forms of media, the birth of Jesus is presented in a familiar narrative. But is the story that gets presented actually the way it occurred in the Bible? Did Mary ride a donkey to Bethlehem? Who was that mean, old innkeeper? Was Jesus born on December 25? This book will try to answer these questions and many more.

The Biblical account of Jesus' birth is found in the books of Matthew and Luke. The two books don't mirror each other, as their stories take place during different times in Jesus' life. Luke focused on the night Jesus was born, while Matthew wrote about the wise men and King Herod, which happened a little later.

There are more than a few differences regarding the traditional Christmas story and the actual Bible story. The Biblical account has been embellished to the point where the Christmas story contains many misconceptions about what truly happened. Embellishments are details added to the Bible that aren't necessarily what the verses say. Misconceptions are views that are either misinterpreted from scripture or are a misunderstanding of the culture from that time period.

The Adoration of the Shepherds
Giovanni Domenico Tiepolo
circa 1751-1753

Over time, the Christmas story has become more dramatic and grandiose. A few changes and enhanced details make for more elaborate and entertaining story-telling. However, the narrative in the Bible is kept simple, giving only the important details. For example, the Bible simply states that Joseph and Mary traveled from Nazareth to Bethlehem. Other sources, like the Disney animated short *The Small One*, build on that, filling in missing details like what their mode of transportation was and the back-story of how it was acquired.

This book is broken down into three parts. Part one gives a short summary of the history of Christmas. Part two addresses some common embellishments and misconceptions about the birth of Jesus, following the narratives of Matthew and Luke using Bible verses from the New International Version. Finally, part three will explore the big question:

Even though December 25 is commemorated as Jesus' birthday by many people, the Bible never mentions Christmas nor instructs us to celebrate it. On the contrary, Jesus told us to remember his death (I Corinthians 11:23-26). He came to save all people from their sins; for all have sinned and come short of the glory of God (Romans 3:23). He was pierced for our transgressions (Isaiah 53:3) and put to death for our sins only to be raised to life for our justification (Romans 4:25). It is only through his death, not his birth, that we can walk in newness of life (Romans 6:4).

PART ONE
THE HISTORY OF CHRISTMAS

Christmas has a history that precedes the birth of Christ, emerging from pagan celebrations. Many holiday icons, like Santa Claus, have origins of a religious nature, while other symbols, like Christmas trees, rose from secular traditions. Even though the Bible did not institute Christmas, those who celebrate it as a religious holiday have incorporated spiritual meanings into most of their customs. Blending many traditions from different cultures over the centuries has developed Christmas into today's holiday.

Santa With Elves
Norman Rockwell
Saturday Evening Post
December 12, 1922
(above)

Helena and Constantine
Vasiliy Sazonov
(right)

Beginning to Look a lot Like Christmas

Why December 25?

The first historical record of Christmas being celebrated on December 25 was in 336 CE (Common Era) during the reign of Emperor Constantine. A few years later Pope Julius I officially decreed that Jesus' birth would be celebrated on the 25th of December.

At the time Christmas was instituted, many European cultures held festivals during the winter solstice. As far back as 217 BCE (Before Common Era), a pagan holiday called Saturnalia was celebrated between December 17th and 23rd. This holiday honored Saturn, the Roman god of agriculture. On December 25th, another festival called Dies Natalis Solis Invicti, translated meaning "birthday of the unconquered sun", was held to honor the sun god, Mithra.

It is a common belief that Christmas was strategically put on December 25 to take the place of those pagan holidays. Replacing the pagan festivals with a new Christian holiday eased the transition of being forcefully converted to Christianity.

Other Dates for Christmas

Some medieval churches celebrated Jesus' birthday on January 6th. That was also the day they celebrated the visit of the wise men and Jesus' baptism. Today, some denominations still celebrate Christmas on this day. In the United Kingdom, January 6th is called "Old Christmas".

At the introduction of the first Christmas holidays, the world was using the Julian Calendar. In 1582, most countries switched to the Gregorian Calendar, which was more accurate and is still in use today. Today, some denominations of Christianity still follow the Julian Calendar. Those that do, celebrate Christmas on January 7. (December 25 on the Julian Calendar is January 7 on the Gregorian Calendar).

Jolly Old Saint Nicholas

Who Was Saint Nicholas?

Santa Claus is well known as the magical bringer of gifts. On Christmas Eve, he flies all over the world in a magic sleigh, bringing presents to the good, little children. The legend of Santa Claus, which has developed over time, can be traced back to a real person called Saint Nicholas. Nicholas was born around 280 CE in the town of Patara, located in modern-day Turkey. He became the bishop of the small, Roman town Myra during a time when the church was greatly persecuted. For his faith, Nicholas spent many years in prison before Emperor Constantine declared Christianity as the official religion of the Roman Empire.

Nicholas was renowned for his generosity and kindness. During his life, he was reported to have given away all his wealth and conducted many acts of charity. Nicholas did most of his alms giving anonymously in accordance with Jesus' teachings in Matthew 6:3-4. Tales of how Saint Nicholas performed miracles and resurrected murdered children are still recited today.

His most famous legend, *Three Impoverished Maidens* or *The Story of The Dowries*, gave birth to the Christmas stocking tradition. The story goes: there was a poor, old man who had three daughters. Since he had nothing to offer for dowries, he wasn't able to find any husbands for his daughters. He feared

what might become of them after he died. Nicholas wanted to help, so under the cover of night, he tossed a bag of money down the chimney and into the poor man's home. The bag landed in a stocking which was hung over the fireplace to dry. After two more nightly visits, the dowries were paid and the three girls were married.

Celebrating St. Nicholas

Saint Nicholas died on December 6 of an unknown year. The anniversary of his death became a day of celebrations. Around 1200 CE, Nicholas became known as the patron saint of children. In folklore, he developed into a magical gift bringer, who gave presents to children on his feast day. He started to take on characteristics of pagan deities, like the Norse god Odin, being depicted with a long white beard and capable of mystical powers, like flight. It was said that he watched over children, making sure they said their prayers and were well behaved.

Through the Renaissance, Nicholas was the most popular saint in Europe. His feast day on December 6 was considered a lucky day and a good time to get married. During the Protestant Reformation in the 16th century, the Catholic saints declined in popularity. Baby Jesus started to be the one to bring gifts to children, which were given on Christmas day instead of December 6. However, Saint Nicholas remained popular in the Netherlands. When Dutch immigrants arrived to the New World colonies, they brought their Christmas traditions with them. In America, the Dutch name for Saint Nicholas, Sinter Klass, turned into the name Santa Claus.

St. Nicholas & the 3 Gold Balls
(depicting the Three impoverished Maidens legend)
Gentile da Fabriano, 1425
(left)

St. Nicholas the Wonderworker
anonymous Russian artist, 1720
National Museum in Warsaw
(above)

Here Comes Santa Claus

In the early 1800s, Saint Nicholas was reintroduced into American pop culture through a series of poems and short stories. In 1809, Washington Irving wrote *Knickerbocker's History of New York,* in which he characterized Nicholas as delivering presents to good children in a flying wagon. Irving called Nicholas the patron saint of New York.

"The Children's Friend," a poem by an anonymous author written in 1821, took away Saint Nicholas' religious affiliation and depicted him wearing a fur coat instead of bishop attire. The writer added more magic to the legend by giving Nicholas a reindeer to pull his wagon.

In 1822, Clement Clarke Moore, an Episcopal minister, wrote a poem called "A Visit from St. Nicholas." It was in this poem, which is also called "The Night Before Christmas," Saint Nicholas was given his flying sleigh pulled by eight flying reindeer. The most familiar attributes associated with Santa Claus were given to him in this story. Moore described St. Nick as a fat, jolly elf who delivered gifts by going up and down chimneys. In 1881, cartoonist Thomas Nast illustrated Moore's poem. Nast was given credit as producing the first images of the modern Santa Claus with a red suit and a workshop at the North Pole.

A Visit From St. Nicholas
Louis Prang (illus.)
1864

Merry Old Santa Claus
Thomas Nast
Harper's Weekly
January 1, 1881

Today, Santa Claus has been stripped of his religious ties to Saint Nicholas, becoming a big secular icon for the holiday. Santa Claus was heavily integrated into the pop culture of America starting in the 1890s when the Salvation Army started using Santa impersonators to solicit donations.

Santa Claus first appeared in motion pictures in the late 1890s. Having started out in short films of the silent movie era, Santa has made it big in Hollywood, staring in numerous holiday blockbusters. Santa has been a staple in the Macy's Thanksgiving Day Parade since the first parade in 1924. By the 1940s, his image started to be used in all sorts of ad campaigns, including World War II propaganda. Newspapers started to use him to advertise the holiday shopping season. Also at that time, stores began to attract children with live Santa Claus impersonators; a tradition that remains popular with small children today.

War Propaganda
circa 1942

The modern depiction of Santa Claus is due, in part, to a series of Coca-Cola advertisements. Although Coca-Cola started using Santa in their campaigns in the 1920s, it was the Sundblom Santa from 1931 that became the standard for the Santa's modern appearance. From 1931 to 1965, artist Hadden Sundblom created holiday themed Coca-Cola ads featuring his version of Santa. The Sundblom Santa was a fully grown white-bearded man, dressed in a red suit with white trim. He wore boots, a large belt, and his iconic Santa hat. This image of Santa, which was kept consistent for over thirty years, shaped how he is depicted and expected to look.

Advertisement
U.S. Confection Co.
1868

Secular Christmas Icons

Many Christmas symbols and customs have pagan origins that date well before the birth of Christ. Most of them originate from pre-Christian western Europe where they were used in festivals during the winter solstice. For example, in pagan mythology, evergreen wreaths symbolized the sun and eternal life. Holly was used to repel evil spirits and celebrate new growth. Yule log traditions began in Nordic ceremonies. When Christianity became the dominant religion in Europe, the church gave these pagan symbols new Christian meanings. For example, holly now represents Jesus' thorn of crowns.

Underneath the Mistletoe

Mistletoe is a parasitic plant that roots itself onto trees. The custom of decorating the inside of houses with mistletoe started with the Celtic Druids, who considered the plant to be sacred. Hanging mistletoe inside was said to bring good luck and ward off evil spirits. The origins of kissing underneath the mistletoe are rooted in Norse mythology.

As legend states, a prophecy foretold that the Norse god Baldur was going to die. To prevent that, his mother, the goddess Frigga, visited all the elements, plants, and animals on Earth and under Earth, making them vow to never harm Baldur. However, she had overlooked mistletoe, which grows on their tree hosts and not on or under the Earth. Loki, the god of mischief, crafted an arrow out of mistletoe and killed Baldur with it. For three days, all of nature tried to bring Baldur back to life. Finally, Frigga was able to resurrect Baldur. The tears Frigga shed for her son turned into the white berries that grow on the mistletoe. In her joy, she kissed everyone who stood under the plant.

In 18th century England, the custom was to pick a berry from the sprig of mistletoe before the kiss was given. After all the berries were plucked, there could be no more kissing under that bough.

O Christmas Tree

In many pagan cultures, evergreen trees were cut down and decorated during winter solstice celebrations, like Saturnalia. The evergreen tree was seen as a symbol of life during the winter. As days were getting shorter, the deciduous trees hibernated and crops died. The pagans viewed evergreens as having mystical powers that allowed them to survive in the winter. During the Saturnalia festival, the Romans adorned their temples with fir trees. The trees were decorated with metal ornaments of their fertility gods and twelve candles to honor their sun god.

According to folklore, the modern Christmas tree is said to have been created by Martin Luther in the 1500s. Legend states, on a night before Christmas, Luther walked through a forest and saw the stars shining through the snow covered trees. It reminded him of Jesus, so he cut down a small fir tree and took it home. He adorned the tree with candles to honor the birth of Jesus on Christmas.

By the 18th century, the Christmas tree tradition was well established in Europe. German immigrants brought the practice to America, where it has become both a secular and Christian symbol of the holiday. For some, the tree became a religious icon that represents Christ's resurrection and a sign for hope. To others, it is just a fun custom.

Under the Mistletoe
Harper's New Monthly Magazine
January 1873
(left)

Family at the Christmas Tree
from a children's book
Netherlands, circa 1860
(above)

Religious Christmas Icons

Christmas celebrations didn't start until the 4th century, so it's not surprising that Christmas is not mentioned in the Bible. No evidence exists in the Bible to indicate that first century Christians celebrated the birth of Christ. However, a few elements from the story of Jesus' birth have been turned into symbols for the holiday.

Angels Heard on High

Many angels are associated with the Biblical account of Jesus' birth. Gabriel, an angel of the Lord, came and told Mary that she would give birth to Jesus (Luke 1:26-38). Another angel of the Lord gave messages to Joseph in his dreams (Matthew 1:20-21, 2:13). After Jesus was born, an angel appeared to shepherds, who were watching their flocks on the outskirts of Bethlehem. The angel told them the wonderful message that the Messiah had been born. After that, he was joined by a multitude of other angels who gave praises unto God.

> *13 And suddenly there was with the angel a multitude of the heavenly host praising God, and saying, 14 Glory to God in the highest, and on earth peace, good will toward men.*
> Luke 2:13-14 (KJV)

Shortly after the Christmas tree was adopted, people would tell their children that the angels decorated the trees. Children were told that tinsel was angel hair that got caught in the branches. In celebrations today, an angel ornament is traditionally used to decorate the very top of the Christmas tree.

Glædelig Jul
Postcard from Norway
circa 1919
(above)

Promotional Card
William B.. Steengerge
Sunshine Publishingn Co.
(right)

Star of Wonder

Another favorite Christmas tree toper is a star ornament, representing the star seen by the wise men. After they had observed the star, they interpreted its appearance as signaling that the Messiah had been born. The wise men made the journey to Judea in order to worship the new born "King of the Jews."

Now when Jesus was born in Bethlehem of Judaea in the days of Herod the king, behold, there came wise men from the east to Jerusalem, 2 Saying, Where is he that is born King of the Jews? for we have seen his star in the east, and are come to worship him. Matthew 2:1-2 (KJV)

Candy Cane Lane

Of course, candy canes aren't mentioned in the Bible. But the myth behind their creation makes candy canes one of the few Christmas symbols that did not originate from a pagan custom.

The first historical records of candy canes don't appear until the 1800s. However, folklore says, in 1670, the candy was created in Cologne, Germany. According to legend, a church choir director gave sugar sticks to the children during the long

Christmas services to keep them quiet. In order to give them Christian significance, the candies were made into the shape of a shepherd's crook to remind the children of the shepherds who visited baby Jesus.

The original candy canes were made completely white, representing Jesus' purity. The red stripes and peppermint flavor weren't added until the turn of the 20th century.

PART TWO
MISCONCEPTIONS AND EMBELLISHMENTS

Every year, the story of Jesus' birth is retold in movies, books, plays, and other formats. The account of the birth of Christ is found in the books of Matthew and Luke. Usually the narrative told at Christmas is presented slightly different than how it is written in the Bible.

Following the birth of Jesus verse by verse, starting with the annunciation to Mary, two kinds of differences will be presented: embellishments and misconceptions. These differences are what separate the Christmas story from the actual Bible story. Embellishments are details added to the narrative that are not expressively stated in the Bible. The Christmas story includes them to enhance it for better storytelling. Misconceptions are elements that are either a misinterpretation of what the scripture says or a misunderstood view of ancient Israeli culture.

Annunciation
Leonardo da Vinci
circa 1472-1475
(above)

Annunciation
Sandro Botticelli
circa 1489
(right)

Annunciation to Mary

Luke 1:26-28

26 In the sixth month of Elizabeth's pregnancy, God sent the angel Gabriel to Nazareth, a town in Galilee, 27 to a virgin pledged to be married to a man named Joseph, a descendant of David. The virgin's name was Mary. 28 The angel went to her and said, "Greetings, you who are highly favored! The Lord is with you."

Who was Gabriel?

Gabriel was an angelic messenger, who had delivered God's word to Daniel (Daniel 9:21) and the priest Zachariah (Luke 1:19). His most famous message was proclaiming to Mary that she was to give birth to the Messiah (Luke 1:26-38). This birth would be miraculous because Mary was a virgin. Gabriel told her that she would conceive through the power of the Holy Spirit and to name the baby "Jesus." The virgin conception was prophesied in the book of Isaiah.

> *Therefore the Lord himself will give you a sign: behold, a virgin shall conceive, and bear a son, and shall call his name Immanuel.* Isaiah 7:14 (ASV)

Under Jewish law, an engagement could be broken if the bride was found to no longer be a virgin. She could lawfully be sentenced to death (Deuteronomy 22:20-21). Joseph, Mary's fiancé, planned to put her away privately (Matthew 1:18-24). But as he thought about it, an angel came to him in a dream and told him that it was alright to take Mary as his wife because she was still a virgin and was being faithful to him.

Mary Visits Elizabeth

Luke 1:39-45

39 At that time Mary got ready and hurried to a town in the hill country of Judea, 40 where she entered Zechariah's home and greeted Elizabeth. 41 When Elizabeth heard Mary's greeting, the baby leaped in her womb, and Elizabeth was filled with the Holy Spirit. 42 In a loud voice she exclaimed: "Blessed are you among women, and blessed is the child you will bear! 43 But why am I so favored, that the mother of my Lord should come to me? 44 As soon as the sound of your greeting reached my ears, the baby in my womb leaped for joy. 45 Blessed is she who has believed that the Lord would fulfill his promises to her!"

The Visitation

After Gabriel left Mary, she went to the hill country of Judea where the priest, Zachariah, and his wife, Elizabeth, lived. At this time, Elizabeth was six months pregnant with John the Baptist. When Mary greeted Elizabeth, John leaped in Elizabeth's womb. Elizabeth was filled with the Holy Spirit and recognized Mary as the mother of the Messiah.

According to Luke 1:56, Mary stayed there for three months before returning home. Not longer after that, Elizabeth was ready to give birth. Eight days after her baby was born, Zachariah, who had been stricken mute by Gabriel as punishment for his unbelief, proclaimed the baby's name by writing on a tablet. After he wrote "his name is John," Zachariah was able to speak again (Luke 1:57-66).

Visitation
Domenico Ghirlandaio
1491
(above)

Bust of Augustus
Mueso Capitolino, Rome
circa 30 BCE
(right)

The Census of Quirinius

Luke 2:1-3
In those days Caesar Augustus issued a decree that a census should be taken of the entire Roman world. 2 (This was the first census that took place while Quirinius was governor of Syria.) 3 And everyone went to their own town to register.

Historical Accuracy:
The Bible is the only historical record of this census. Historians have documented evidence to prove that Quirinius didn't become governor until after King Herod died. Because of this, many people point to the census of Quirinius to prove that the Bible is historically inaccurate. Here are four plausible explanations to rectify the apparent discrepancy.

1. Roman censuses were taken regularly and often took many years to complete. It could have been that this census was still being conducted as Quirinius took office.

2. Historians agree that Quintilius Varus was the governor before Quirinius took over around 6 or 7 CE. Quirinius was a strong military leader who may have been put in charge of Israel during Varus' reign because of the Jews' rebellious nature against Roman rule.

3. A Latin inscription discovered in 1764 has been interpreted to indicate that Quirinius served as governor on two occasions.

4. Luke 2:2 says, *This was the first census that took place while Quirinius was governor of Syria.* However, this could also be translated "This census took place before Quirinius was governor of Syria." That would require translating the Greek word *protos* as *before* instead of *first,* which is plausible.

Embellishment: Mary's Donkey

Luke 2:4-5

4 So Joseph also went up from the town of Nazareth in Galilee to Judea, to Bethlehem the town of David, because he belonged to the house and line of David. 5 He went there to register with Mary, who was pledged to be married to him and was expecting a child.

Did Mary Ride a Donkey?

The Bible simply states Joseph and Mary went to Bethlehem in order to register in the census. It does not mention what mode of transportation they were using. The Bible also doesn't say if they traveled with anyone else, like the way they traveled with many relatives and friends in Luke 2:44. Since Mary was pregnant, it could very well have been that she traveled by donkey or rode in a cart. However, the Bible is mute on the subject, so it can't be certain.

> *And [Joseph] saddled the ass and set [Mary] upon it; and his son led it, and Joseph followed.*
> The Protevangelium of James 17:5

The notion that Mary rode a donkey comes from an apocryphal gospel called the Protevangelium of James. This book was dated to circa 145 CE, which was much later than the four gospels in the Bible. Among other things not found in the Bible, the Protevangelium of James asserts that Joseph was an elderly man who had children from a previous marriage.

The donkey that Mary was supposed to have ridden has become a major character in many Christmas stories. He has been given multiple names and personalities. Some well known stories include the Rankin-Bass film *Nestor the Long Eared Christmas Donkey* and Disney's *The Small One*.

Misconception: The Urgency

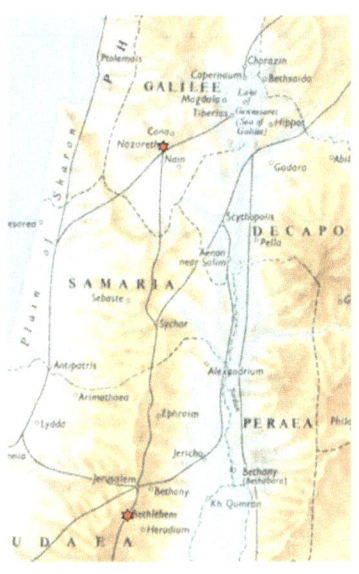

Luke 2:6
While they were there, the time came for the baby to be born

Nazareth to Bethlehem
Nazareth is approximately 70 to 80 miles from Bethlehem. Mary and Joseph most likely traveled along the plains by the Jordan river and then through the hill country of Judea. Even though the average person could complete the journey in about five days, since Mary was pregnant, it is likely they would have taken longer.

When Did They Arrive?
Every nativity play or movie seems to tell of how Mary and Joseph made it to Bethlehem just as Mary went into labor. Having Mary arrive in the nick of time packs in more drama and condenses the story down for better story-telling. But this is not how it is presented by the scriptures.

> *And so it was, that, while they were there, the days were accomplished that she should be delivered.*
> Luke 2:6 (KJV)

According to the Bible, Mary and Joseph were already in Bethlehem before the time came for the baby to be born. It doesn't say how long there were there before Mary went into labor. It simply states that while they were there the time came for Jesus to be born. There is no indication of any urgency, unlike in Luke 1:39 and 2:16 when Mary and the shepherds, respectively, "hurried" on their way.

Journey to Bethlehem
mosaic at Chora Church
Istanbul, Turkey
(left)

Misconception: No Room at the Inn

Luke 2:7

and she gave birth to her firstborn, a son. She wrapped him in cloths and placed him in a manger, because there was no guest room available for them.

Was there an Inn?

A typical Christmas play usually depicts Mary and Joseph arriving in Bethlehem just as Mary is about to have the baby. As they try to seek refuge at an inn, the grumpy innkeeper tells them there is no room and sends them away. However, the Bible makes no mention of a disgruntled innkeeper or any part of this encounter.

> The King James Version of Luke 2:7 reads:
> *And she brought forth her firstborn son, and wrapped him in swaddling clothes, and laid him in a manger; because there was no room for them in the inn.*

The original Greek word that caused this misconception is *kataluma*. The King James translators were not consistent in translating this word into English. *Kataluma* should not have been translated as *inn*. The more appropriate translation is *guest room*, which is how it appears in newer Bible translations. The King James translators correctly translated *kataluma* as *guest chamber,* when it was used to describe the Upper Room in Luke 22:11 and Mark 14:14.

There is a Greek word for a public inn, which is *pandokheion*. Luke, when writing his gospel, used that word in Luke 10:34 as the location where the Good Samaritan took the wounded man. *Pandokheion* is the word Luke used for a hotel type inn and *kataluma* was used to describe the guest room of a house.

Traveling and Hospitality

In those days, when people traveled, it was customary for the travelers to stay with family members. Such was the case when Mary traveled to Judea and stayed with her cousin, Elizabeth (Luke 1:56). Since Joseph was traveling back to his hometown, it is highly likely he had extended family there who would have provided him with a place to stay.

Hospitality was a big part of the Jewish culture. It was a command under the Law of Moses to show hospitality to foreigners (Leviticus 19:33-34). The Bible contains many examples of people showing hospitality. Abraham invited three of God's messengers, into his home and ministered to them (Genesis 18). A Shunammite woman and her husband had an extra room built especially for Elisha to stay when he was in town (II Kings 4). Mary and Martha hosted Jesus and his disciples in their house (Luke 10); as did the owner of the Upper Room (Mark 14). In Matthew 25:31-46, Jesus told a parable about what doing good deeds unto others means to him.

The Biblical town of Bethlehem was a tiny village. It had a small population and there were no major Roman roads going through it. It is unlikely that this village would even have contained a public inn like the one in the Christmas story.

The Night Before the Birth of Christ
Michael Rieser
1869
(left)

Herbergssuche
Carl Rahl (attr)
1865
(above)

Misconception: Born in a Barn

Ancient Israeli Architecture

Remember, *kataluma* was the name for the guest room of a house. A typical Israeli house was two stories and was mostly made of stone. The *kataluma* (guest room) as well as the rest of the living quarters were on the upper level. The ground level, underneath the living area, contained the animal shelters. The family's animals were brought into the lower section of the house at night to keep them safe from the cold, predators, and thieves. Their body heat warmed the house. Only wealthy people could afford to build stables and barns.

There is mention of animals being housed indoors in other parts of the Bible. I Samuel 28:24 tells of a woman who had a calf inside her house. The judge, Jephthah, promised to sacrifice the first thing that came out of his house as a burnt offering in Judges 11:31. He was probably expecting an animal to come out of his house when he made that promise.

According to Kenneth Bailey, a Middle Eastern Scholar, "It is we in the West who have decided that life with these great gentle beasts is culturally unacceptable. The raised terrace on which the family ate, slept and lived was unsoiled by the animals, which were taken out each day and during which time the lower level was cleaned. Their presence was in no way offensive."[1]

Because the living quarters in the upper level of the house were all full, Mary and Joseph had to take a room on the ground level which usually housed the animals.

Israelite Pillared House
circa 900 BCE (model)
Nick Laarakkers, 2007

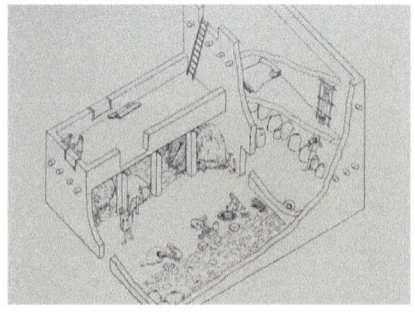

Four Room House (diagram)
Israel Museum, Jerusalem
Chamberi, 2013

Misconception: The Wooden Manger

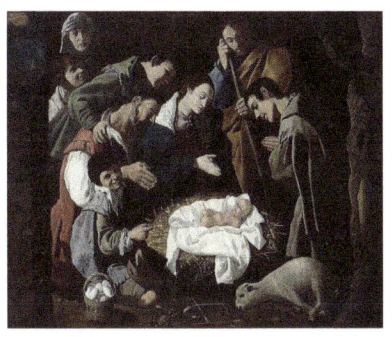

What was a Manger?

The manger is usually depicted as a wooden feeding box, filled with hay. However, archaeological findings tell us that most mangers, as well as Israeli houses and furniture, were crafted out of stone. Stone was the most common material used for construction, since stone was a more abundant resource than lumber. Clay was the second most common material used to build mangers

In Matthew 13:55, Joseph was called a *tekton*, a Greek word usually interpreted as *carpenter*. The literal definition of *tekton* was *craftsman* or *builder*. It was a general term for any craftsman who worked not just with wood, but also stone, clay, or metal. Joseph could have worked with wood but he was most likely a mason who built things out of stone.

Israeli flocks and herds were left to graze and were not grain fed. With the majority of animals having a grass based diet, mangers mostly functioned as water troughs. They were custom built to suit the heights of the animals using them.

The wooden, hay filled mangers seen at Christmas were likely the result of blending the Bible story with the European and western cultures that originated the holiday and used those kinds of mangers.

[1] Bailey, K. (2007, Fall). The Manger and the Inn: The Cultural Background of Luke 2:7. *Bible and Spade*, p. 105.

Adoration of the Shepherds
José de Sarabia (attr.)
1630
(top)

Stone trough from Megiddo
circa 900 BCE
seetheholyland.net
(bottom)

Embellishment: Singing O'er the Plain

Luke 2:8-15

8 And there were shepherds living out in the fields nearby, keeping watch over their flocks at night. 9 An angel of the Lord appeared to them, and the glory of the Lord shone around them, and they were terrified. 10 But the angel said to them, "Do not be afraid. I bring you good news that will cause great joy for all the people. 11 Today in the town of David a Savior has been born to you; he is the Messiah, the Lord. 12 This will be a sign to you: You will find a baby wrapped in cloths and lying in a manger."

13 Suddenly a great company of the heavenly host appeared with the angel, praising God and saying, 14 "Glory to God in the highest heaven, and on earth peace to those on whom his favor rests." 15 When the angels had left them and gone into heaven, the shepherds said to one another, "Let's go to Bethlehem and see this thing that has happened, which the Lord has told us about."

Angels at Jesus' Birth

At Christmas time, there are many nativity scenes that include an angel positioned above baby Jesus. It is true that Luke wrote about angels, but the Bible never says that any were present at the manger scene. The angels' role on the night of the birth of Christ was to proclaim to the shepherds that Jesus was born. After they appeared to the shepherds, the angels returned back into heaven.

Hark! The Herald Angels Sing

Many Christmas carols reference how the angels sang praises to God. It might make for some beautiful songs, but the Bible doesn't say the angels sang or were singing. The scripture says the angels were "praising God and saying" (Luke 2:13).

Embellishment: The Cattle are Lowing

Luke 2:16-20

16 So they hurried off and found Mary and Joseph, and the baby, who was lying in the manger. 17 When they had seen him, they spread the word concerning what had been told them about this child, 18 and all who heard it were amazed at what the shepherds said to them. 19 But Mary treasured up all these things and pondered them in her heart. 20 The shepherds returned, glorifying and praising God for all the things they had heard and seen, which were just as they had been told.

Were Animals Really There?

The Bible states that Jesus was placed into a manger, but it does not mention if any animals were present. The tale of oxen and lambs keeping time for a drummer boy is completely fictitious. Since Mary and Joseph were staying in the manger room, animals may have been there. On the other hand, the animals may have been removed while Mary gave birth.

In addition to the shepherds, Joseph's other family members as well as midwives could have been there. After the shepherds saw Jesus, they went and spread the word to other people who then probably came to see Jesus too. However, this is all speculation, since the Bible doesn't say.

Animals in the Nativity Scene

The history of the nativity scene started with paintings from the 2nd century CE, which depict animals being present. Saint Francis of Assisi was given credit as having made the first living nativity scene in 1223 CE. His nativity scene included a live donkey and ox. After preaching next to it, the hay from his manger was reported to have developed miraculous healing powers. It wasn't until 65 years after St. Francis that the first stone, clay, and wood nativity figurine sets started to appear. The tradition of including not only animals but angels and the wise men continues today.

Angels Announcing the Birth of Christ to the Shepherds
Govert Flinck, 1639

Jesus' Circumcision

Luke 2:21

On the eighth day, when it was time to circumcise the child, he was named Jesus, the name the angel had given him before he was conceived.

Why was Jesus Circumcised?

In the 17th chapter of Genesis, God made a covenant with Abraham, promising to make his descendants into a great nation with kings coming through his lineage. As a sign of this covenant, God required Abraham and all of his male descendants to be circumcised. Circumcision of male babies was a requirement to the Israelites under the Law of Moses.

And in the eighth day the flesh of his foreskin shall be circumcised.
Leviticus 12:3 (ASV)

Since Jesus was a Jew, he was circumcised on his eighth day. It was customary to name the baby at the circumcision ritual. Eight days after he was born, Mary and Joseph named their baby Jesus, the name given to them by the angels in Luke 1:31 and Matthew 1:21. John the Baptist was also circumcised and named when he was eight days old (Luke 1:59-63).

The Circumcision
Workshop of Giovanni Bellini
circa 1500
(above)

Presentation of Christ at the Temple
Hans Holbein the Elder
circa 1500
(right)

The Purification Rites

Luke 2:22-24

22 When the time came for the purification rites required by the Law of Moses, Joseph and Mary took him to Jerusalem to present him to the Lord 23 (as it is written in the Law of the Lord, "Every firstborn male is to be consecrated to the Lord", 24 and to offer a sacrifice in keeping with what is said in the Law of the Lord: "a pair of doves or two young pigeons."

Why Did They Go to the Temple?

Under the Law of Moses, two things were required from a woman after she gave birth. First, she had to go through a period of ceremonially uncleanness. According to Leviticus chapter 12, if a woman had a boy, she was ceremonially unclean for seven days. On the eighth day, the boy was circumcised. After that, she had to wait thirty-three days before she could be purified. If she had a daughter, she had an even longer period of ceremonially uncleanness.

Second, after the period of uncleanness was over, she had to give a lamb as a burnt offering and a dove or pigeon as purification offering. If the mother was too poor to afford a lamb, she could offer two doves or pigeons. This was what Mary had to do.

Mary and Joseph had one extra thing to do at the temple. Since Jesus was Mary's first born son, he had to be presented to God. Exodus 13:1-2 required every firstborn, both human and animal, to be concentrated to the Lord. God declared every first born son belonged to Him. Those born to humans and unclean animals could be redeemed from God, but those born to cows, goats, and sheep had to be offered as sacrifices. The process for redeeming a firstborn son can be found in Numbers 18:14-19.

Simeon

Luke 2:25-35

25 Now there was a man in Jerusalem called Simeon, who was righteous and devout. He was waiting for the consolation of Israel, and the Holy Spirit was on him. 26 It had been revealed to him by the Holy Spirit that he would not die before he had seen the Lord's Messiah. 27 Moved by the Spirit, he went into the temple courts. When the parents brought in the child Jesus to do for him what the custom of the Law required, 28 Simeon took him in his arms and praised God, saying:

29 "Sovereign Lord, as you have promised, you may now dismiss your servant in peace. 30 For my eyes have seen your salvation, 31 which you have prepared in the sight of all nations: 32 a light for revelation to the Gentiles, and the glory of your people Israel."

33 The child's father and mother marveled at what was said about him. 34 Then Simeon blessed them and said to Mary, his mother: "This child is destined to cause the falling and rising of many in Israel, and to be a sign that will be spoken against, 35 so that the thoughts of many hearts will be revealed. And a sword will pierce your own soul too."

Who was Simeon?

While Mary and Joseph were at the temple, they were met by Simeon, who was described as being righteous and devout. God had promised him that he would see the Messiah before he died. After seeing Jesus, Simeon praised God and declared that Jesus would be the salvation for the people of every nation.

Simeon wasn't called a prophet, but he did make a prophecy to Mary, saying that a figurative sword would pierce her soul. This came to pass as Mary watched her son die on the cross (John 19:25-27).

Anna and the Return to Nazareth

Luke 2:36-40

36 There was also a prophet, Anna, the daughter of Penuel, of the tribe of Asher. She was very old; she had lived with her husband seven years after her marriage, 37 and then was a widow until she was eighty-four. She never left the temple but worshiped night and day, fasting and praying. 38 Coming up to them at that very moment, she gave thanks to God and spoke about the child to all who were looking forward to the redemption of Jerusalem.

39 When Joseph and Mary had done everything required by the Law of the Lord, they returned to Galilee to their own town of Nazareth. 40 And the child grew and became strong; he was filled with wisdom, and the grace of God was on him.

Who was Anna?

After being blessed by Simeon, Mary and Joseph met Anna, who was identified as a prophetess. She was an elderly widow who was continually worshiping in the temple. After she saw Jesus, she instantly recognized him as the Messiah. Then, she started to proclaim it to everyone around her in the temple. After the encounters with Simeon and Anna, Mary and Joseph continued with their sacrifices.

Luke's story of Jesus' birth ends with Joseph and Mary returning to Nazareth after the sacrifices were completed. This book does not record the story of the wise men's visit, King Herod, or the flight into Egypt. Those are found in Matthew.

Simeon in the Temple
Rembrandt van Rijn, 1628
(left)

The Presentation in the Temple
Ambrogio Lorenzetti, 1342
(above)

Embellishment: We Three Kings

Matthew 2:1-6

After Jesus was born in Bethlehem in Judea, during the time of King Herod, Magi from the east came to Jerusalem 2 and asked, "Where is the one who has been born king of the Jews? We saw his star when it rose and have come to worship him." 3 When King Herod heard this he was disturbed, and all Jerusalem with him. 4 When he had called together all the people's chief priests and teachers of the law, he asked them where the Messiah was to be born. 5 "In Bethlehem in Judea," they replied, "for this is what the prophet has written:

6 "'But you, Bethlehem, in the land of Judah, are by no means least among the rulers of Judah; for out of you will come a ruler who will shepherd my people Israel.'"

Who Were the Wise Men?

The Bible says wise men, or Magi, came to visit Jesus; they are never called kings. The wise men are only found in the book of Matthew, which doesn't record their names, ages, or ethnic backgrounds. They brought three gifts with them, but the actual number of men who came is unknown. The only clue to their country of origin was that they came to Jerusalem from the east. Even though the Bible contains little information about who the Magi actually were, many Christian groups have devised their own traditions regarding the identities of the wise men.

The Magi of Tradition

In Christianity overall, there is no consensus about who the Magi were. This is due to their identities not being established in scripture. The majority of traditions say there were three wise men, due to the number of gifts they gave. However, some Eastern churches, especially the Syraic Church, say there were twelve wise men. A variety of different names and ethnicities are given to the Magi, depending on the region and beliefs of a given denomination. For example, churches in China believe that one wise man was Chinese.

Typical America tradition names three wise men. The first and oldest was Gasper from Tarsus. He was 60 years old with a long, white beard, who brought the gold. Melchior from Arabia was the second. He was 40 years old and gave frankincense. The final wise man was Balthazar from Africa, who was 20 years old and had dark skin. He brought myrrh.

The ages and ethnicity of these traditional wise men were carefully selected. Their ages, 20, 40, and 60, represent the three ages of the adult man. They were given backgrounds to incorporate three different geographical regions and cultures.

Adoration of the Magi
Raphael
circa 1504
(left)

Adoration of the Magi
Jan de Bray
1674
(above)

Misconception: Magi at the Birth

Matthew 2:7-8

7 Then Herod called the Magi secretly and found out from them the exact time the star had appeared. 8 He sent them to Bethlehem and said, "Go and search carefully for the child. As soon as you find him, report to me, so that I too may go and worship him."

The Magi in the House of Herod
James Tisso 1886-1894

When Did They Get There?

Many nativity scenes contain more wise men than shepherds. However, the Bible does not say the Magi were there on the night Mary gave birth. In fact, the scriptures seem to indicate that they did not arrive until some time after.

The Bible does not tell precisely when the wise men came to visit Jesus, however, it does give some clues. In Matthew 2:7, the wise men tell King Herod the exact time that the star appeared. Then in Matthew 2:16, Herod killed all the male babies two years old and under in accordance with that time the wise men gave him. It is inferred from this that the Magi arrived much later than the night of Jesus' birth. It is likely that they didn't get to Bethlehem until up to two years later.

Matthew only referred to Jesus a *child,* unlike Luke who intermixed the words *baby* and *child.* This could suggest Jesus was a toddler at the time. On the other hand, Matthew never calling Jesus a baby doesn't necessarily mean he wasn't one. Also, Matthew 2:11 says the wise men came into the house to see Jesus. The lack of the manger could suggest that Joseph and Mary had moved out of the lower level of the house and were now living in the proper living quarters on the second story.

The tradition of including the wise men into the nativity scene was likely a result of blending Luke's and Matthew's account of Jesus' birth together.

Misconception: Following Yonder Star

Stern von Bethlehem
Waldemar Flaig, 1920

Matthew 2:9-11

9 When they had heard the king, they set out; and there, ahead of them, went the star that they had seen at its rising, until it stopped over the place where the child was. 10 When they saw that the star had stopped, they were overwhelmed with joy.

When Did the Star Move?

It is commonly believed the wise men saw the star in their country and followed the it all the way to see Jesus. However, the Bible doesn't present the story that way. According to Matt 2:2, the wise men came to Jerusalem after only just seeing the star. The star isn't recorded to have moved until they left Jerusalem and were traveling on their way to Bethlehem.

Analyzing Matthew 2:9

"When they had heard the king"- After they saw the star and recognized that it meant the Messiah was born, they traveled to Jerusalem to search for the new born "King of the Jews". If the star was leading them on their entire journey, why would it take them to Jerusalem when Jesus was in Bethlehem?

"They set out"- After they heard the prophecy that the Messiah would be born in Bethlehem, the wise men left Jerusalem. Bethlehem is a short trip, between five and six miles, from Jerusalem.

"And there, ahead of them, went the star that they had seen at its rising"- This was when the star started moving in the sky. It was then the wise men actually used the star like a GPS and followed it as it went across the sky.

"Until it stopped over the place where the child was"- The star showed the wise men the exact location where Jesus was. The wise men were joyful when they found Jesus' house.

What is Frankincense and Myrrh?

Matthew 2:11

On entering the house, they saw the child with Mary his mother; and they knelt down and paid him homage. Then, opening their treasure chests, they offered him gifts of gold, frankincense, and myrrh.

Gifts Fit for a King

The wise men brought three gifts to Jesus: gold, frankincense, and myrrh. Two of these are mentioned in the book of Isaiah as being lavish gifts going to be given to Israel by kings from other nations.

> *The multitude of camels shall cover thee, the dromedaries of Midian and Ephah; all they from Sheba shall come; they shall bring gold and frankincense, and shall proclaim the praises of Jehovah.* Isaiah 60:6 (ASV)

According to the Biblical Archeology Society, gold, frankincense, and myrrh were valuable items presented to honor kings and deities. Gold was inherently valuable as a precious metal, frankincense was an expensive perfume or incense, and myrrh was an anointing oil. Some ancient inscriptions reveal that these three items were offered to the Greek god Apollo in 243 BCE by King Seleucus II Callinicus.[2]

Frankincense is the resin of the Boswellia sacra tree native to Africa

Myrrh is the resin from the Commiphora tree native to Yamen

Symbolic Significance

Scholars and theologians have tried to interpret the significance of these gifts by applying special spiritual meanings to them. The gold represented Jesus' kingship. Jesus was given the title "Lord of lords and King of kings" (Revelation 17:14). He built a spiritual kingdom of which he said "is not of this world" (John 18:36). Those who are a part of the Church are in his kingdom. According to Colossians 1:18, Jesus is the head of the Church and reigns supreme in all things.

Frankincense, an incense, represented his priesthood. In Jewish worship, priests would offer incense to God. Zachariah was conducting an incense offering when Gabriel appeared to him. Jesus' sacrifice was called a "fragrant offing and sacrifice to God" in Ephesians 5:2. The Hebrews writer said Jesus has a permanent priesthood because he lives forever (Hebrews 7:24). That passage goes onto say:

> *Unlike the other high priests, he does not need to offer sacrifices day after day, first for his own sins, and then for the sins of the people. He sacrificed for their sins once for all when he offered himself.* Hebrews 7:27

The myrrh, which was commonly used for embalming the dead, foreshadowed Jesus' death. In Mark 15:23, while hanging on the cross, Jesus was offered wine mixed with myrrh to drink. Before Joseph of Arimathea and Nicodemus buried Jesus' body, they anointed it with a sizable mixture of aloes and myrrh (John 19:38-41).

[2] Biblical Archeology Society Staff. (2013, December 9). *Why Did the Magi Bring Gold, Frankincense and Myrrh?*

High Priest Offering Incense on the Alter
from *Treasures of the Bible*
by Henry Davenport Northrop, 1894
(above)

Embellishment: Many Babies Were Slain

Matthew 2:12-18

12 And having been warned in a dream not to go back to Herod, they returned to their country by another route. 13 Now after they had left, an angel of the Lord appeared to Joseph in a dream and said, "Get up, take the child and his mother, and flee to Egypt, and remain there until I tell you; for Herod is about to search for the child, to destroy him." 14 Then Joseph got up, took the child and his mother by night, and went to Egypt, 15 and remained there until the death of Herod. This was to fulfill what had been spoken by the Lord through the prophet, "Out of Egypt I have called my son."

16 When Herod saw that he had been tricked by the wise men, he was infuriated, and he sent and killed all the children in and around Bethlehem who were two years old or under, according to the time that he had learned from the wise men. 17 Then was fulfilled what had been spoken through the prophet Jeremiah: 18 "A voice was heard in Ramah, wailing and loud lamentation, Rachel weeping for her children; she refused to be consoled, because they are no more."

The Massacre of Innocents

After the wise men left, Joseph was divinely warned in a dream to flee to Egypt with his family. King Herod was planning on killing this new "King of the Jews", which was why he had told the Magi to return to Jerusalem and tell him where Jesus was staying. In Herod's mind, he was the only King of the Jews and Jesus threatened that kingship.

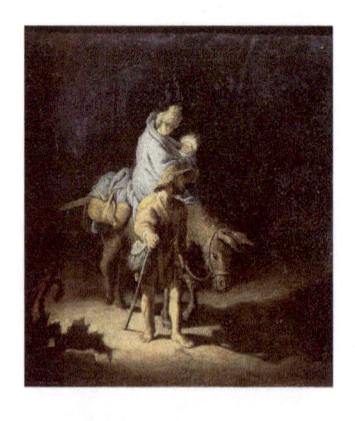

Fortunately, the wise men were warned in a dream not to return to Herod, so the king never found out where Jesus was. Herod's solution to that problem was to kill all the male children under two years old in Bethlehem. Little did he know, Jesus escaped and was safe in Egypt.

How Many Infants Died?

In the Christmas story, the number of infant deaths is usually exaggerated, most likely to show how evil King Herod was. In reality though, since Bethlehem was a very small village, it would stand to reason that not very many children were killed.

The Bible doesn't give the exact number of babies that were slain. Matthew 2:16 says Herod killed *all* the male children in and around Bethlehem who were two years old and under. (Newer translations omit "male"). However, *all* doesn't necessarily mean *a lot*. The Bible is the only historical record of this event taking place. It is recorded in the Bible because Herod's actions directly affected Jesus and also fulfilled prophecy (Jeremiah 31:15). Since the massacre of innocents was ignored by secular historians, it is likely that not many Bethlehemites fell victim to Herod's execution order.

The exaggeration is likely the result of comparing Jesus' life to Moses. During the time Moses was born, the Egyptian Pharaoh saw that the Hebrew people were multiplying in great numbers. He decreed that if a Hebrew son was born, that baby must be killed (Exodus 1:8-22). Both stories tell of a king who gave orders for the execution of male babies, but the number of Pharoah's victims was much greater than King Herod's.

The Flight into Egypt
Rembrandt van Rijn
1627
(left)

Massacre of the Innocents
Peter Paul Rubens
circa 1609-1611
(above)

PART THREE
When Was Jesus Born?

Determining the precise time of Jesus' birth is a highly debatable subject. Multiple studies by numerous theologians and historians have brought little consensus. The Bible does not say what year Jesus was born, however, careful analysis of scripture can give some clues. In the mist of multiple theories and estimations that exist, the following material will build a timeline of events, trying to stay consistent with both historical and Biblical records.

The calendar used in the Bible was the Hebrew calendar. This was a lunar calendar, meaning it followed the cycles of the moon instead of the sun. Each of the twelve Hebrew months began on a new moon. During the time of Jesus' birth, the modern day Gergoiran calendar was not in use. This makes it complicated to pinpoint an accurate modern date for these events. To avoid confusion, only dates from the Hebrew calendar will be presented. In this system, ten lunar months would equal a typical forty week pregnancy term.

Hebrew months in relation to the modern calendar (above)

Census to Collect the Tax Before Quirinius mosaic at Chora Church Istanbul, Turkey (right)

Was Jesus Born in December?

The Census

The census described in Luke 2:1-3 required everyone to travel to their ancestral hometown. Although Luke's account is the only historical record of this census being taken, all the other censuses conducted during this time period were never done in the winter. In winter months people were less able to travel due to freezing temperatures and poor road conditions. Taking this into account, Jesus probably couldn't have been born in a winter month like December.

Also, since it was customary to tax citizens at the time of a census, it was likely after the fall harvest. The major crops were in after the harvest, so people were more able to travel and the farmers would have had the bulk of their income.

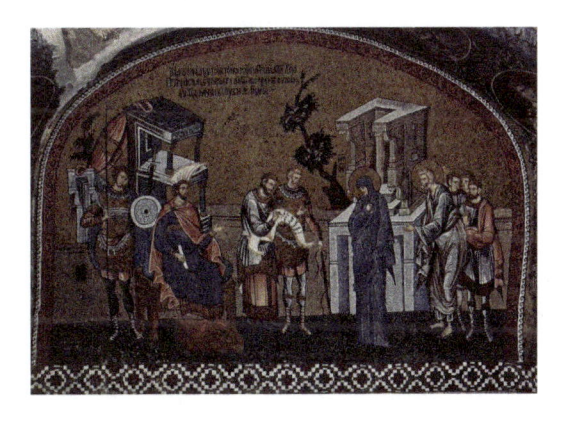

Shepherds in the Fields

Luke 2:8 says the shepherds were out in the fields with their flocks at night time. It was customary to send the sheep out to the wilderness around the time of Passover and bring them in at the commencement of the first rain. During the time they were out in the fields, shepherds watched them night and day. During the rainy season and the winter months, the sheep were corralled, especially at night.

Passover took place in the first Jewish month, Nisan, and the first rains came in the eighth month, Heshvan. Since the shepherds were still out in the fields at night, it have to have been sometime between these two months.

The Seventy Weeks Prophecy

Daniel 9:24-27

24 "Seventy 'sevens' are decreed for your people and your holy city to finish transgression, to put an end to sin, to atone for wickedness, to bring in everlasting righteousness, to seal up vision and prophecy and to anoint the Most Holy Place.

25 "Know and understand this: From the time the word goes out to restore and rebuild Jerusalem until the Anointed One, the ruler, comes, there will be seven 'sevens,' and sixty-two 'sevens.' It will be rebuilt with streets and a trench, but in times of trouble. 26 After the sixty-two 'sevens,' the Anointed One will be put to death and will have nothing. The people of the ruler who will come will destroy the city and the sanctuary. The end will come like a flood: War will continue until the end, and desolations have been decreed. 27 He will confirm a covenant with many for one 'seven.' In the middle of the 'seven' he will put an end to sacrifice and offering. And at the temple he will set up an abomination that causes desolation, until the end that is decreed is poured out on him."

The Seventy Weeks Prophecy

The Seventy Weeks Prophecy was the name given to a prophecy from the book of Daniel. While the prophet Daniel was praying, the angel Gabriel appeared him. Gabriel delivered this prophecy which was ultimately about Jesus, referring to him as "the Anointed One."

The year in which Jesus was born can be calculated by analyzing this passage in the book of Daniel. Although interpreting the prophecy can be rather tricky, the result is that Jesus was born in 4 BCE. When the modern calendar was created, the plan was to start counting years from the birth of Christ. Therefore, it would be expected that Jesus would have been born in 1 CE. However, during the implementation of the calendar, his birth year was miscalculated, which threw it off by four years.

Determining Jesus' Birth Year

Interpreting the Prophecy

The Hebrew word for *weeks* was *shabua* which means "sevens." There were 70 "sevens" in the prophecy, which meant 70 seven year periods of time. This made a total of 490 years. The first 69 *shabuas* were split into 7 (49 years) and 62 (434 years). Then the final *shabua* (7 years) was cut short exactly in the middle.

The starting point of when the 70 weeks started was in verse 25: a decree to rebuild Jerusalem. This came about in the rein of the Persian emperor Artaxerxes I in 457 BCE. In Ezra chapter 7, the decree was given and Ezra, along with other Israelites, moved back to Israel from Babylon. 49 years later, Jerusalem was fully rebuilt.

Starting with 457 BCE and adding 49 years made it 408 BCE. Adding the remaining 434 years brought it to 27 CE, the year Jesus started his ministry.

According to verse 27, the anointed one would die exactly in the half way point of the 70th *shabua*. One prophetic week equaled seven years, so the half way point would be three and a half years. This was how long Jesus' ministry lasted before he died in 31 CE. Since Luke 3:23 stated that Jesus was about 30 years old at the start of his ministry (27 CE), and since there was no zero year, it would make the year of his birth 4 BCE.

Angel of the Annunciation
Franciabigio
circa 1510s

Abijah: The Starting Point

Where to Start?

The Bible doesn't say exactly when Jesus was born. However, it does give a starting point for figuring out an estimated time. Scripture indicates John the Baptist was roughly six months older than Jesus. So, an educated guess can be made if the date of John's birth can be calculated. According to the seventy weeks prophecy as well as consensus among historians, Jesus was born in 4 BCE. Since Jesus had to have been born between Passover and the first rains, John had to have been conceived in the first half of 5 BCE. The key to figuring out when John was conceived is found in Luke.

> *There was in the days of Herod, king of Judaea, a certain priest named Zacharias, of the course of Abijah: and he had a wife of the daughters of Aaron, and her name was Elisabeth.*
> Luke 1:5 (ASV)

What is Abijah?

Zachariah, John's father, was a priest who was a member of the priestly division of Abijah. According to I Chronicles 24:6-19, Abijah was the eighth out of twenty-four divisions. The divisions rotated weeks of service in the temple. In a normal Hebrew year, there were fifty-one weeks. Each division did two, nonconsecutive weeks of service. All the divisions had to work three extra weeks during Passover, Pentecost, and Tabernacles.

According to Luke 1:8, Zachariah was serving in the temple when Gabriel appeared to him. Because John had to have been conceived in the first half of 5 BCE, this visitation would have occurred in Abijah's first week of service in the spring.

The Hebrew year began on the 1st of Nisan. Abijah would have served during the 2nd week for Passover, the 9th week for Pentecost, and the 10th week for their division specific week of service. The 10th week of service would have started on the second Sabbath day of the 3rd month, Sivan. Zachariah would have returned home after the third Sabbath of Sivan.

Estimating Jesus' Birthday

Constructing a Timeline

Gabriel appeared to Zachariah between the second and third Sabbaths of Sivan and struck Zachariah mute at this time. Zachariah lived in the hill country of Judea, which wasn't far from Jerusalem. His wife, Elizabeth, would have conceived by the end of Sivan and remained in seclusion for five months (Luke 1:23-24).

Six months into Elizabeth's pregnancy, in the ninth month, Kislev, Gabriel appeared unto Mary and she conceived Jesus. Mary hurried to Elizabeth's house and spent the winter there (Luke 1:56). After three months, she returned to Nazareth. The month of Nisan would have been the tenth and final month of Elizabeth's pregnancy. Elizabeth gave birth to a baby boy. Eight days later, the baby was named John and Zachariah could speak again.

Months passed and then Mary went down to Bethlehem for the census. If Mary became pregnant in Kislev, it would mean Jesus was born forty weeks (or ten lunar months) later in the seventh month, Tishri. Eight days after his birth, Jesus was circumcised and named. Thirty-three days after the circumcision, Mary went to the temple to give sacrifices.

This time frame lines up with Luke's account, as the shepherds would still have been out in the fields in Tishri. It also would have been after the fall harvest when the census would likely have been conducted.

Zecharias and Gabriel
unnamed artist
circa 1800
(left)

The Birth of John the Baptist
Jacopo Tintoretto
1554
(above)

Could It Have Been A Holiday?

The Holy Days

Just because Jesus wasn't actually born on Christmas doesn't mean that he couldn't have been born on a holiday. In fact, many events surrounding John the Baptist and Jesus' births seem to line up with select Jewish holy days. Whether or not those events actually happened on those holy days is debatable, but here is some evidence supporting it.

John: the New "Elijah"

John the Baptist was conceived toward the end of the third month, Sivan. Moving forward forty weeks (ten lunar months), the length of a typical pregnancy, would make it the first month, Nisan, which contains the Jewish holy day of Passover. Passover was established in Exodus chapter 12, and commemorated how God freed the Israelites from Egyptian bondage. During Passover it was (and still is) customary to set out a special cup of wine in anticipation of the arrival of Elijah. This is based on a prophecy given by Malachi:

> *Behold, I will send you Elijah the prophet before the great and terrible day of Jehovah come.* Malachi 4:5

Before John was born, the angel who foretold his birth told Zachariah that John would possess the spirit and power of Elijah (Luke 1:17). In Matthew 17:10-13, Jesus explained to his disciples that John the Baptist was the "Elijah" that the Jews were expecting to come. Passover begins on the 15th day of Nisan, making this a likely birth date for John, the expected "Elijah."

John the Baptist
Preaching before Herod
Pieter Fransz de Grebber
circa 1600-1653

Jesus: the Light of the World

If John's conception took place late in the third month, Sivan, it would mean that Mary became pregnant six months later in Kislev. It is interesting that the Festival of Lights began on the 25th of Kislev. The Festival of Lights, or Hanukkah was an eight day long festival that commemorated the re-dedication of the temple. According to the story, for eight days the temple's menorah miraculously stayed lit even though there was only enough fuel for one day.

In his writings, John called Hanukkah the feast of dedication (John 10:22). Twice in the Gospel of John, Jesus is cited as calling himself the "light of the world" (John 8:12, 9:5). Later in that gospel, when he was teaching, Jesus again referred to himself as a light:

> *I am come a light into the world, that whosoever believeth on me may not abide in the darkness.* John 12:46 (ASV)

Did Gabriel visit Mary during Hanukkah? Could Jesus, the "light of the world," have been conceived on the Festival of Lights? It can't be known for certain, but it is a possibility.

God With Us

If John was born on the 15th of Nisan and was six months older than Jesus, that means Jesus could have been born on the 15th of Tishri, which signaled the start of the festival of Tabernacles. The Feast of Tabernacles, also called Sukkot, was one of the three festivals that required all men to travel to Jerusalem to observe them (the other two being Passover and Pentecost). This festival was a time of rejoicing and a celebration of Israel's deliverance from Egyptian slavery.

> *Therefore the Lord himself will give you a sign: behold, a virgin shall conceive, and bear a son, and shall call his name Immanuel.* Isaiah 7:14 (ASV)

In addition to being called "the Light of the World," Jesus was also called Immanuel, which means "God with us." Jesus, the Son of God, came down to Earth to dwell (or tabernacle) with his people. As John wrote:

> *And the Word became flesh, and dwelt among us (and we beheld his glory, glory as of the only begotten from the Father), full of grace and truth.* John 1:14 (ASV)

The Greek word that was translated into "dwelt" in this verse is *skénoó*. This is not the common Greek word for "dwelt". *Skénoó* literally means "tabernacled". John described how Jesus took on a physical body in order to tabernacle with his people on Earth.

During the Feast of Tabernacles, Israelites would build a sukkah; which was a temporary shelter made from tree branches. They would live in them during the celebration as a reminder of how their ancestors lived in the wilderness after being delivered out of Egypt. The festival was a foreshadow of the time when God would tabernacle with His people on Earth. Much like how the presence of God resided in the tabernacle in Old Testament times, God made a sukkah of flesh in the body of Jesus.

The 15th of Tishri in the year 4 BCE corresponds with October 6th on the Julian calendar. After converting this date to the modern Gregorian calendar, it would equate to the 4th of October. It is recorded in the Gospel of Luke that Jesus' birth took place at night. Since a Hebrew day was from sunset to sunset, it is possible that Jesus was born either after dusk on October 3rd or after midnight on October 4th. Could Tishri 15th, the Feast of Tabernacles, be day the Word was made flesh and began to tabernacle among us?

Shemini Atzeret

Jesus was circumcised on his eighth day, in accordance with the Law of Moses. The Feast of Tabernacles was a seven day long celebration. A new holiday, called Shemini Atzeret, occurred on the eighth day. This holy day was celebrated on the 22nd of Tishri and was considered separate from the Feast of Tabernacles.

According to Leviticus 23:36-39, it was to be a day for a solemn assembly of the people and was considered a sabbath day. *Shemini Atzeret,* when translated, literally means "the assembly of the eight (day)". If Jesus had been born on the first day of the Feast of Tabernacles, his circumcision would have taken place on Shemini Atzeret.

Sukkah Meal
Bernard Picart
1722
(above)

The Death of King Herod

When Did Herod Die?

Emil Schürer (1844 – 1910) was a German scholar who wrote about the history of the Jews. He proposed that King Herod died in 4 BCE, which has remained the consensus among historians. However, his claim has been challenged in recent times, and there is evidence to conclude that King Herod really died later than 4 BCE.

Josephus

When he had done these things, he died, the fifth day after he had caused Antipater to be slain; having reigned, since he had procured Antigonus to be slain, thirty-four years; but since he had been declared king by the Romans, thirty-seven. The Antiquities of the Jews 17:8:1

According to *The Antiquities of the Jews* by first century Jewish historian Flavius Josephus, Herod died thirty-seven years after he was appointed to be king by the Romans. Elsewhere in his records, Josephus said that Herod was appointed as king in the consulship of Calvinus and Pollo, which began in late 40 BCE and ended in 39 BCE. Proponents of the 4 BCE death year start counting the thirty-seven years Herod reigned from 40 BCE, but this was not how Josephus counted his years.

A new king could begin his reign at any given time during the year and wouldn't have ruled for an entire year that year. Josephus did not count the partial first year as a king's first year in office. He started with their first complete year. Using Josephus' records as well as Roman historians Appian and Dio Cassius, it's indicated that Herod came to power in 39 BCE. Therefore, Josephus would have started recording Herod's kingship from 38 BCE; Herod's first full year in office. Thirty-seven years later would be 1 BCE.

The Eclipse

Elsewhere in Josephus' records, he states that Herod died between a lunar eclipse and Passover. Proponents of the 4 BCE death year cite a partial lunar eclipse that took place twenty-nine days before Passover that year. However, in 1 BCE there was a full lunar eclipse that took place in Tevet, eighty-nine days before Passover. Josephus also recorded the things Herod did during the period between the eclipse and Passover.

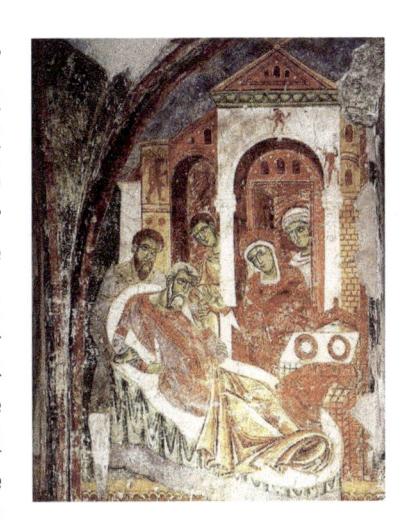

According to biblical historian Andrew E. Steinmann, author of *From Abraham to Paul: A Biblical Chronology:* "all of the events that happened between these two [the eclipse and passover] would have taken a minimum of 41 days had each one of them taken place as quickly as possible. A more reasonable estimate is between 60 and 90 days"[3]

Herod would have needed at least forty-one days to do all the things he was recorded to have done. The time between the eclipse and Passover in 4 BCE wasn't enough, but the elapsed time in 1 BCE was. Also, it is more likely that Josephus would have recorded a full eclipse as opposed to a partial one in terms of a reference point. This all suggests that Herod died sometime between the Tevet eclipse and the Passover of Nisan, 1 BCE.

[3] Steinmann, A. (2011) *From Abraham to Paul: A Biblical Chronology.* St. Louis, MO. Concodia Publishing House, p. 231

wood engraving of Josephus from *The Works of Flavius Josephus* (1854 edn) William Whiston (trans) (left)

The End of King Herod fresco at Benedictine Church Lambach, Austria (above)

Timeline of the Birth of Jesus

Sivan (June), 5 BCE
Annunciation to Zachariah
Between the second and third Sabath of Sivan Gabriel came to Zachariah in the temple. Elizabeth became pregnant shortly afterward.
Luke 1:5-25

Nisan (April), 4 BCE
Birth of John the Baptist
After three months, Mary returned home. In Nisan, Elizabeth was in her 10th an final month of pregnancy and gave birth to John the Baptist.
Luke 1:56-66

Kislev (December), 5 BCE
Annunciation to Mary
Six Hebrew months into Elizabeth's pregnancy, Gabriel appeared to Mary. Mary became pregnant and went to visit Elizabeth.
Luke 1:26-45

Tishri (October), 4 BCE
Birth of Jesus
Mary gave birth to Jesus in Bethlehem, where they were visited by the shepherds. Eight days later, Jesus was circumcised and named.
Luke 2:1-21

Circa 2 BCE
Adoration of the Magi
Approximately two years after Jesus was born, he was visited by the wise men. King Herod sought to kill Jesus, but Joseph fled with his family to Egypt.
Matthew 2:1-18

Tevet (January) - Nisan (April), 1 BCE
Death of King Herod
During this period, King Herod died. After which, Joseph and his family returned to Nazareth.
Matthew 2:19-23

Heshvan (November), 4 BCE
Presentation in the Temple
41 days after Jesus was born (33 after he was circumcised), Joseph and Mary presented him in the temple and conducted sacrifices.
Luke 2:22-40

Conclusion

There have been various other dates and years assigned to Jesus' birth and the death of King Herod. Even though it is hoped that the material presented in this book is accurate to the historical events, they may very well be incorrect. The precise date of the birth of Christ will forever remain a mystery.

What's not a mystery is that the Savior really was born. It does not matter if the exact date or the minor details of his birth are known. Celebrating the birth of Jesus is not found nor commanded in the Bible. It is far more important to understand the reason why he left his place in Heaven to be born on Earth.

Jesus was God, who was made manifest in the flesh (I Timothy 3:16). As the angel told Joseph in Matthew 1:21, Jesus came to "save his people from their sins." Our salvation and hope was made possible by his death, not his birth. What matters is that he was condemned to die only to rise again triumphantly. He offered himself as a perfect sacrifice to free us from our burdens of sin.

> *"He himself bore our sins" in his body on the cross, so that we might die to sins and live for righteousness; "by his wounds you have been healed."* I Peter 2:24

It is through Jesus' sacrifice and God's wonderful grace, we can some day join Him in Heaven. His grace is a gift given to those who are faithful and follow His word. He did this because of his love for us (John 3:16).

> *For by such grace you have been saved through faith. This does not come from you; it is the gift of God.* Ephesians 2:8

When we are baptized, we are buried into Christ's death and rise again to walk in a new life, just as Jesus was risen through the glory of God. Through baptism, we are united with Jesus and have been set free from sin, becoming an instrument of righteousness (Romans 6:1-14).

Through his sacrifice, Jesus has given the entire world the gift of eternal life and he wants to give it to you. There is only one simple way to receive it:

HEAR so you may BELIEVE the Gospel message.
> *So then faith cometh by hearing, and hearing by the word of God.* Romans 10:17 (KJV)

> *How then shall they call on him in whom they have not believed? and how shall they believe in him of whom they have not heard? and how shall they hear without a preacher?* Romans 10:14 (KJV)

REPENT from your sins, so that you may be forgiven.
> *Repent ye therefore, and be converted, that your sins may be blotted out, when the times of refreshing shall come from the presence of the Lord;* Acts 3:19 (KJV)

CONFESS your belief that Jesus is the Christ, the Son of God.
> *32 Whosoever therefore shall confess me before men, him will I confess also before my Father which is in heaven. 33 But whosoever shall deny me before men, him will I also deny before my Father which is in heaven.* Matthew 10:32-33 (KJV)

Be BAPTIZED for the forgiveness of sins.
> *Then Peter said unto them, Repent, and be baptized every one of you in the name of Jesus Christ for the remission of sins, and ye shall receive the gift of the Holy Ghost.* Acts 2:38 (KJV)

Live a FAITHFUL LIFE
> *be thou faithful unto death, and I will give thee a crown of life.* Revelation 2:10d (KJV)

Bibliography

Abrahamus. (2010, November 30). *HCSBSB: Iron Age Israelite Home.* Retrieved from Guild of Bezalel: http://guildofbezalel.blogspot.com/

Akin, J. (2013, April 17). *Jesus' birth and when Herod the Great *really* died.* Retrieved from National Catholic Register: http://www.ncregister.com

Akin, J. (2013, April 13). *The 100-year old *mistake* about the Birth of Jesus.* Retrieved from JimmyAkin.com: http://jimmyakin.com/

Answers in Genesis. *Christmas, No Room for and Inn, Visit of the Magi.* Retrieved from Answers in Genesis: https://answersingenesis.org/holidays/christmas

Bailey, K. (2008, November 8). *The Manger and the Inn.* Retrieved from Associates for Biblical Research: www.biblearchaeology.org

Bailey, K. (2007, Fall). The Manger and the Inn: The Cultural Background of Luke:2:7. *Bible and Spade*, p. 105.

Biblical Archaeology Society Staff. (2013, December 9). *Why Did the Magi Bring Gold, Frankincense and Myrrh?* Retrieved from Bible History Daily: http://www.biblicalarchaeology.org/

Biblical Magi. Retrieved September 30, 2014, from Wikipedia, the free encyclopedia: http://en.wikipedia.org/wiki/Biblical_Magi

Bulkeley, T. (2007). *Agriculture.* Retrieved from Hypertext Bible Commentary - Amos: http://www.bible.gen.nz/

Callahan, A. (2013, November 21). *The Legend of Coca-Cola and Santa Claus.* Retrieved from Coca-Cola: http://www.coca-colacompany.com/holidays/

Catholic Encyclopedia: Magi. (2014, September 30). Retrieved from New Advent: http://www.newadvent.org/

Chaffey, T. (2012, March 16). *Popular Conservative Journalist Attacks Genesis and the Birth of Christ.* Retrieved from Answers in Genesis: https://answersingenesis.org

Church of God Study Forum. (2012, January 20). *Hebrew/Roman Calendar Comparison.* Retrieved from Church of God Study Forum: http://www.cgsf.org/dbeattie/calendar/

Coca-Cola Converstions Staff. (2012, January 1). *The True History of the Modern Day Santa Claus.* Retrieved from Coca-Cola: www.coca-colacompany.com/holidays/

Cooper, J. (2014). *Christmas Traditions & Customs.* Retrieved October 18, 2014, from whychristmas?com: http://www.whychristmas.com/customs/

Cooper, J. *Why is Christmas Day on the 25th December?* Retrieved from whychristmas?com: http://www.whychristmas.com/

Coppersmith, M. J. (2014). *Christmas: A Real World Christmas Luke 2:1-7.* Retrieved from Preaching: http://www.preaching.com/sermons/

Fletcher, E. *Houses & Tents.* Retrieved October 1, 2014, from Bible Archaeology: http://www.bible-archaeology.info/housing.htm

Francis, Z. T. *Christmas Symbols and Their Meanings.* Retrieved from A Christmas Testimony: http://www.achristmastestimony.kingdomdesignministry.com/

Handwerk, B. (2013, December 20). *St. Nicholas to Santa: The Surprising Origins of Mr. Claus*. Retrieved from National Geographic: http://news.nationalgeographic.com/

History Channel. (2013, December 24). *Why do we kiss under the mistletoe?* Retrieved from Ask History: http://www.history.com/news/ask-history/

History.com Staff. (2010). *Santa Claus*. Retrieved from History: http://www.history.com/topics/christmas/santa-claus

Hopler, W. (2014). *The History of Christmas Tree Angels*. Retrieved from About Religion: http://www.about.com/religion

Huie, B. T. (1997, August 22). *WAS THE "LAST SUPPER" THE PASSOVER MEAL?* Retrieved from Here a Little, There a Little: http://www.herealittletherealittle.net/

Is St. Nicholas a Real Saint? Retrieved October 2014, from St. Nicholas Center: http://www.stnicholascenter.org/

Jewish Encyclopedia. (1901-1906). Retrieved from http://www.jewishencyclopedia.com/

JewishRoots.Net. (2013-2015). *Was the Birth of Our Messiah During the Feast of Tabernacles*. Retrieved from JewishRoots.Net: https://jewishroots.net

Josephus, F. (1737). *Antiquities of the Jews*. William Whiston (trans).

Nuwer, R. (2012, December 14). *The First Nativity Scene Was Created in 1223*. Retrieved from SMITHSONIAN.COM: http://www.smithsonianmag.com/

Padfield, D. (2013). *Away In A Manger...* Retrieved from Bible Land History: http://www.biblelandhistory.com/

Porter, J. (2007). *Jesus Christ*. Oxford, NY: Oxford University Press.

Reid, J. O. (1994, December). *When Was Jesus Born?* Retrieved from Church of the Great God: http://www.cgg.org

Religion News Service. (1995, December 23). *A Long, Cold Road to Bethlehem*. Retrieved from Los Angeles Times: http://articles.latimes.com/

Ritenbaugh, R. T. (1994, December). *Seventy Weeks Are Determined...* Retrieved from Church of the Great God: http://www.cgg.org/

Robinson, B. (2000, December 29). *All about the Christmas Tree: Pagan origins, Christian adaptation, & secular status*. Retrieved from Religious Tolerance: http://www.religioustolerance.org/

Scheifler, M. *What Day was Jesus Born?*. Retrieved September 15, 2015 from Bible Light: http://biblelight.net/sukkoth

Steinmann, A. (2011) *From Abraham to Paul: A Biblical Chronology*. St. Louis, MO. Concordia Publishing House, p. 231

Seiglie, M., & Robinson, T. (20012, November-December). Was There Really "No Room in the Inn"? *The Good News A Magazine of Understanding*, pp. 28-31.

Spinner, J. (2010, December 14). *What Is Frankincense?* Retrieved from Slate: http://www.slate.com/

Taylor, P. S. (2013). *What are some of the most common misconceptions about Jesus Christ's birth?* Retrieved from Christian Answers.Net: http://christiananswers.net/christmas/

The 70 Weeks of Daniel. (2009). Retrieved from Daniels 70 Week Prophecy: http://www.Daniels70Weeks.com

The Protevangelium of James. In *The Apocryphal New Testament.* Oxford: Clarendon Press. (1924).

Three Impoverished Maidens or The Story of The Dowries. Retrieved October 2014, from the Saint Nicholas Center: http://www.stnicholascenter.org/

Witcher Goldstein, L. *The History of the Candy Cane.* Retrieved October 2014, from Noel Noel Noel: http://www.noelnoelnoel.com/trad/candycane.html

Witherington III, B. (2013, February 12). *Mary, Simeon or Anna: Who First Recognized Jesus as Messiah?* Retrieved from Bible History Daily: http://www.biblicalarchaeology.org/

Bible Verses

All Bible verses, unless otherwise noted, are from the New International Version, used under fair use clause: less than 500 verses and 25% content. All verses were retrieved from: https://www.biblegateway.com

Holy Bible, American Standard Version. (1900). Public Domain.

Holy Bible, King James Version. (1611). Public Domain.

Holy Bible, New International Version. (2011). Biblica, Inc.

Picture Credits

All images, unless otherwise stated, are copyright free and/or in the public domain and were retrieved from Wikimedia Commons: http://commons.wikimedia.org/wiki

Four Room House. (2013, May 5). Chamberi. Retrieved from Wikimedia Commons: http://commons.wikimedia.org/wiki/File:Four_room_house._Israel_Museum,_Jerusalem.JPG used under the Creative Commons Atteibution-Share Alike license

Frankincense. (2005, December 31). Snotch. Retrieved from Wikimedia Commons: http://commons.wikimedia.org/wiki/File:Frankincense_2005-12-31.jpg photograph released into the Public Domain by author

Grotto of the Nativity (Stone Trough). (2010, November 24). Seetheholyland.net. Retrieved from Flickr: https://www.flickr.com/photos/seetheholyland/5205311705/ no modifications made, used under public license

Israelite Pillared House. (2007, January 18). Nick Laarakkers. Retrieved from Wikimedia Commons: http://commons.wikimedia.org/wiki/File:Israelite_pillared_house.jpg used under the terms of the GNU Free Documentation License

Myrrh. (2005, September 14). Gaius Cornelius. Retrieved from Wikimedia Commons: http://commons.wikimedia.org/wiki/File:Myrrh.JPG photograph released into the Public Domain by author

Palestine in Jesus Times (Map). Public Domain. Retrieved from http://www.biblesnet.com/maps.html

Lightning Source UK Ltd.
Milton Keynes UK
UKHW050816270519
343376UK00008B/335/P